A STEP-BY-STEP BOOK ABOUT
TROPICAL MARINE
AQUARIUM FISHES

DR. C.W. EMMENS

Photography: Dr. Gerald R. Allen, Dr. Herbert R. Axelrod, K.H. Choo, Helmut Delbelius, Douglas Faulkner, U. Erich Friese, Michael Gilroy, Michio Goto, Hilmar Hansen (Aq. Berlin), Burkhard Kahl, Rudie Kuiter, Ken Lucas (Steinhart Aq.), Gerhard Marcuse, Arend van den Nieuwenhuizen, Hans and Klaus Paysan, Dr. Dwayne Reed, Dr. Shih-Chien Shen, Roger Steene, Robert P.L. Straughan, P. Terver, G. Wolfsheimer, Dr. Fujio Yasuda.

Humorous Drawings: Andrew Prendimano.

Distributed in the UNITED STATES by T.F.H. Publications, Inc., One T.F.H. Plaza, Neptune City, NJ 07753; in CANADA to the Pet Trade by H & L Pet Supplies Inc., 27 Kingston Crescent, Kitchener, Ontario N2B 2T6; Rolf C. Hagen Ltd., 3225 Sartelon Street, Montreal 382 Quebec; in CANADA to the Book Trade by Macmillan of Canada (A Division of Canada Publishing Corporation), 164 Commander Boulevard, Agincourt, Ontario M1S 3C7; in ENGLAND by T.F.H. Publications Limited, Cliveden House/Priors Way/Bray, Maidenhead, Berkshire SL6 2HP, England; in AUSTRALIA AND THE SOUTH PACIFIC by T.F.H. (Australia) Pty. Ltd., Box 149, Brookvale 2100 N.S.W., Australia; in NEW ZEALAND by Ross Haines & Son, Ltd., 82 D Elizabeth Knox Place, Panmure, Auckland, New Zealand; in the PHILIPPINES by Bio-Research, 5 Lippay Street, San Lorenzo Village, Makati Rizal; in SOUTH AFRICA by Multipet Pty. Ltd., Box 235, New Germany, South Africa 3620. Published by T.F.H. Publications, Inc. Manufactured in the United States of America by T.F.H. Publications, Inc.

Contents

Fishes developed in the sea and only later invaded fresh waters. Yet, for obvious reasons, aquarists kept freshwater fishes long before they had any success with marines. Our present day successes have been made possible by a cluster of developments that include better aquarium construction, high

INTRODUCTION

quality artificial sea water, adequate filtration techniques, adequate and rapid transport, and reasonable disease control. The availability of fishes on which to practice our newly developed skills has largely depended on scuba and similar diving methods—if we ignore the undesirable use of poisons seen in some parts of the world.

The sea houses two main groups of fishes, the cartilaginous fishes, whose skeleton has relatively little calcium, and the bony fishes, with rigid, highly calcified skeletons. Nearly all aquarium specimens are bony fishes, since the cartilaginous ones are characteristically large, unattractive and predatory. So are many bony fishes, but there are many hundreds of species of small and attractive fishes, and these are the ones we keep. Most come from coral reefs, but by no means do all. We have not yet developed techniques for breeding marine fishes on a commercial scale, or indeed on any scale, beyond a few species that show some degree of promise. In contrast to freshwater species, many of which are aquarium or pond bred, nearly all of our specimens are caught in the wild.

What sort of places have they come from? Those in the majority have come from a shallow part of the ocean, much of

Facing Page: The sea houses many beautiful fishes. Some of the most popular among hobbyists are the butterflyfishes; these fishes are brightly colored and come in a wide variety of patterns. In this photo are: *Chaetodon plebius, C. trifasciatus,* and *C. zanzibariensis.*

it well lit; otherwise the reef-building corals would not thrive. The coral area is also well aerated by waves breaking over the top of the reef. There is an abundance of animal and vegetable food and hiding places for the fishes. The temperature may be as high as 84°F (29°C) and, near the surface, the water may be diluted from heavy rain (but a few feet down this will not be felt). At low tide, the uppermost corals may be exposed. This limits the growth of the reef. The reef slopes seaward, often quite steeply, until it gives way to a sandy bottom or to formations occupied by creatures that need no bright illumination.

Fish Populations

Although the reefs and shoals may seem crowded with fish, they are a part of a vast ocean and encounter new water all the time. In public aquaria, this is simulated by the use of a large water reserve to continually purify the sea water as it is circulated. In your aquarium, conditions are different and it will

Lighting is very important in the marine aquarium, and a wide selection of bulb types is available.

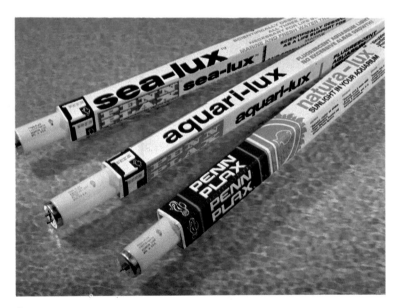

Give your fishes plenty of room, which means plenty of water; ammonia toxicity in salt water is over ten times the amount it is in fresh water. Shown here are the anemone demoiselle, *Amphiprion ocellaris*, and the blue devil, *Chrysiptera cyanea*.

not be possible to crowd the fishes in the same way or in the way that freshwater fishes can be crowded. You will be circulating the water, but only through equipment of limited efficiency, and most of the water will be in the aquarium at any one time. Conditions resembling the tropical ocean impose other restrictions. A high temperature and a high pH of 8.0-8.4 (degree of alkalinity) mean that the oxygen content of the water is low and that the toxicity of ammonia is high. Ammonia is the main break-down product of the fish metabolism and of any decaying material in the water. Ammonia is a chief cause of trouble in the aquarium. Compared with a freshwater tank at pH 7.0 (neutral), the saltwater tank is exposed to over ten times the toxicity of a given amount of ammonia.

All this means that your fishes must be given plenty of room, not less than five gallons (20 liters) of water for a small fish averaging two inches (five cm) in length. They will have a good appetite due to the high temperature (78°-84°F; 24°-29°C) but must not be fed too liberally or they will pollute the water. Luckily, fishes convert around 50% of their food to good use, as against our 10% or so. So what seems to us a meager diet is ample for a fish as long as it is nutritious.

SUCCESS

There is more than one way of starting a successful marine aquarium. Some are fairly simple and inexpensive set ups, others employ complex equipment and can cost a lot. The expensive ones are usually claimed to be almost foolproof and time saving, but the more equipment you have, the more there is to go wrong.

Almost any system needs a running-in period, except the old-fashioned "sterile" method that uses purely physical and chemical purification techniques. This is because others all use biological filtration in one form or another to get rid of ammonia by breaking it down to relatively harmless nitrates or nitrogen gas by bacterial action. There are several ways of running-in a tank and they all take some time—several weeks at least. It is useless to be impatient, so read up on the subject and get started along the right lines.

A healthy aquarium implies healthy fishes. Since these will come from the wild, there is a high probability that they

Clean water is essential to most all marine fishes. Many tanks are filtered with several different filters, each specializing in a specific type of filtration. To determine the best filtration system for your tank, talk with your local pet store owner.

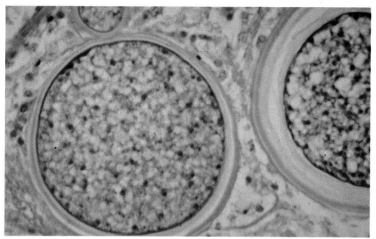

Spores of the fungus *Ichthyosporidium hoferi* in the liver of a saltwater fish.

will carry disease. They may not be sick, but it is very likely that there will be a few white spots or velvet infections unnoticeable or unseen because they are on the gills. Unless a new fish has already been quarantined, it is wise to treat it for these potential troubles. If you are going to keep only fishes, it can be done in the aquarium when you first add the fishes and at each subsequent addition, as long as they are not too frequent. Otherwise, quarantine must be in a separate tank, set up like the main tank, but smaller and with few decorations.

Quarantine can also take the form of passive observation and then transfer to the main aquarium after three or four weeks if all seems well. Luckily, marine white spot and velvet are both curable by treatment with copper; many aquarists use it. Some add formalin to the treatment, others give each fish a one- or two-minute bath in fresh water as well; this kills off many surface infestations. I find the latter rather heroic and prefer just a simple copper treatment. In these circumstances, a two-week quarantine is sufficient as long as nothing untoward turns up. With copper, the biological filter will not be seriously affected, nor will it remove the copper rapidly, but a carbon filter must be turned off.

DISEASES

Velvet, or coral fish disease, is characterized by fishes glancing off objects in the aquarium, respiring rapidly, and likely having clamped fins. On close inspection, they may be seen to have a white powdery dusting on the body surface, hard to see except in oblique illumination. The cause is *Amyloodinium ocellatum*, a protozoan that settles on the gills and body surface after a free-swimming stage and forms cysts that produce more free-swimming young. Treatment with copper sulphate or citrate should continue for at least ten days; maintain a concentration of 0.15 parts per million (ppm or mg per liter). Copper is removed from solution very readily in sea water and becomes attached to the substrate or coral; therefore, the concentration must be monitored with a copper kit. If no kit is used, one-half doses added at two-day intervals will probably be sufficient and remain below the toxic level to fishes, which starts at about 0.4 ppm.

There are many test kits on the market today. Be sure when you purchase your kit that it is one specifically for salt water testing.

Devices for measuring various water qualities range from electrical through colorimetric, and there are many different types of products designed to change the chemical composition of water in the marine tank. Check with your pet dealer for sound advice about testing and adjusting your aquarium's water.

White spot is another gill and skin infection. It is caused by the protozoan, *Cryptocaryon irritans*. Like velvet, it has a free-swimming stage when it is most easily killed. The free-swimming tomites settle on the fish and develop into white cysts up to ½5 inch (one mm) in diameter. These irritate the fish and cause a behavior similar to velvet. Treatment with copper is indicated as above.

Bacterial diseases can result in red streaks on the body or fins that if untreated can result in ulceration and fin or tail rot (parts dropping off). Many species of bacteria may be the cause, and treatment is best undertaken by feeding an antibiotic (as long as the fishes are eating). Mix chloromycetin (chloramphenicol) for preference, or any other wide-spectrum antibiotic at about 1% with a flake or other suitable food and feed twice daily. If the fishes are not eating, treat the whole tank with 50-100 mg per gallon (four liters) of the antibiotic and turn down the biological filter. Do not use aureomycin, which froths and turns red.

Tuberculosis is caused by *Mycobacterium marinum*. Infected fishes waste away with various degenerative signs such as hollow belly, ragged fins, and ulcerated skin. Get rid of affected fishes for preference, as treatment is prolonged. If you decide to treat the disease, the drug to use is isoniazid, fed to the fishes as for antibiotics or added to the water at 40 mg per gallon (four liters), repeated every third day with a 25% water change. A cure may take up to two months.

Cysts of one sort or another are usually caused by spore-forming protozoa and are not curable in our present state of knowledge. Common causative organisms are *Henneguya, Plistophora* and *Glugea* species.

The only fungal infection of note in marine fishes is *Ichthyosporidium (Ichthyophonus) hoferi*, a slow-spreading organism that attacks the liver and kidneys and later spreads everywhere. Its first visible appearance is as brown cysts breaking through the skin. No certain cure is available and affected

Pet shops and tropical fish specialty stores stock a variety of remedies designed specifically for use in treating diseases of marine aquarium fishes.

Introduction

One way to determine the relative health of your fish is to note the intensity of the coloration they display. Here is a coral beauty, *Centropyge bispinosus*, showing its gorgeous colors.

fishes are best disposed of, although some fishes may limit the disease and live on indefinitely.

Flukes are an occasional nuisance, the most common being *Benedenia melleni*. It settles on the skin or gills and grows to about ⅙ inch (four mm), causing distress and even open wounds. Treatment is difficult; the best results recently reported have been with the pesticides Dibrom, Dipterex, and Dylox (all contain Trichlorfon) at 0.25 ppm (0.25 mg per liter). They are stirred into a gallon (four liters) of tank water and gradually added to the aquarium. The same treatment may be tried for fish lice *(Argulus)* and copepods.

13

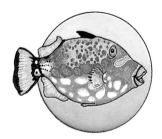

You are going to see more species of marine fishes in aquarium shops than I shall describe here, but you will soon recognize most of them as being related to one or other of those I do describe. This will give you a clue to their suitability and requirements. Those I talk about are most al-

FISHES

ways available although not always suited to a medium-sized community aquarium. Of course, you cannot expect to see them all in a pet shop at any one time, but you can expect to come across them sooner or later or to be able to order them from your dealer unless otherwise indicated.

Pomacentridae

This is a large family of small fishes that includes the demoiselles or damselfishes and the anemonefishes, often called clownfishes. They are usually regarded as beginners' fishes since most of them are hardy and easy to keep. However, with some exceptions, it is usually not advisable to keep more than one member of each species unless in a large aquarium, when shoals may be kept together.

The blue chromis *(Chromis cyanea)* and the blue-green chromis *(C. caeruleus)* are exceptions to the rule just stated and may also be kept in schools if desired. They swarm in masses on the reef and present a fantastic sight. The males build nests and guard the eggs until they hatch—and are then quite liable to feast on the young. Both species are omnivorous and will eat almost anything, live or otherwise.

Facing Page: The powder blue surgeonfish, *Acanthurus leucosternon*, is an exceedingly attractive fish with an interesting manner of swimming.

Pomacentrus coelestis, a blue damselfish, will add a touch of brilliance to your tropical marine aquarium.

The black-tailed humbug *(Dascyllus melanurus)* and the white-tailed humbug *(D. aruanus)* are so alike in appearance and behavior that they were hardly distinguished at first. A black or white tail is all that differentiates them, although *D. aruanus* does tend to be a bit chunkier than *D. melanurus*. Both are almost anemonefishes, in that they often swarm among the tentacles of the large tropical anemones but do not inhabit them permanently. They are very hardy and easy to feed. There are quite a number of other pretty *Dascyllus* species worth keeping. They are easy to feed and keep but are often quite pugnacious. The worst is *D. trimaculatus*, the three-spot damsel fish; he grows quite large and should be avoided.

Two blue damselfishes *(Pomacentrus coelestis* and *Abudefduf cyanea)* and a yellow-tailed blue *(P. melanochir)* are well worth having, adding a touch of bright color to the aquarium. Some very brilliant blues come from the Philippines and

Fishes

there is a plethora of different species also available. Generally speaking, other members of the genus *Abudefduf* are fairly dull, even the famous sergeant major *(A. saxatilis)*; but, two species are spectacular, the sapphire devil *(A. cyaneus)* and the black velvet damselfish *(A. oxydon)*.

The genus *Amphiprion* contains the anemonefishes, on the whole less hardy than the damsels, but mostly hardy enough even for a beginner. Curiously, the commonly offered clown anemonefish *(A. ocellaris)*, known for a long time as *A. percula*, a more colorful fish, is not the hardiest by any means. Yet it is one of the few marine fishes that has been bred commercially, with both parents caring for the eggs rather like the freshwater cichlids. If you buy *A. ocellaris*, it can be kept in schools, with or without an anemone, but must be handled carefully during transfer to the new tank. Take your time over this and all should be well.

Dascyllus trimaculatus, the three-spot damsel; it tends to be territorial and is often pugnacious.

The yellow-tailed anemonefish *(A. clarkii)* is a good species to keep with an anemone, as it is one of the best feeders of its host, taking chunks of food too large for it to eat itself and thrusting them into the anemone. The saddle anemonefish *(A. ephippium)* and the red clown *(A. frenatus)* are rather scrappy but very tough and ready to spawn in the aquarium. I had an inter-specific "pair," a male *frenatus* and a female *ephippium*, that spawned over 100 times at approximately fortnightly intervals in a community tank, with occasional rest periods of two or three months. Another easily kept member of the genus is the skunk clown *(A. akallopisos)*, a yellow fish with a white-striped back.

The spine-cheeked anemonefish *(Premnas biaculeatus)* is a beauty. However, it can grow rather large, up to about six

The yellow-tailed anemonefish, *Amphiprion clarkii*, will help feed its host.

The red clown, *Amphiprion frenatus*, is a rather scrappy but very hardy fish.

inches (15 cm), and rather pugnacious; yet, unless it is a dominant fish in the tank, it is often attacked by others. Difficult, but it is worth keeping! The male is smaller than the female, who often loses her attractive white stripes as she grows; unfortunately, sex is not apparent in the young fish.

Labridae

The wrasses or labrids are characterized by their peculiar way of swimming, for when undisturbed they row themselves along with the pectoral fins. If they feel like it, they can shoot through the water just like any other fish, only faster, using the body muscles and tail. They are carnivorous by choice but will take some vegetable matter. They are easy to keep. They have a disconcerting habit of burying themselves in the gravel and when first placed in the aquarium may lie on their sides, but they soon settle in.

The red labrid *(Coris gaimard)* shows a characteristic of many of the labrids, a change in pattern as it grows, going from a white-spotted, red juvenile to a blue-spotted adult quite different in pattern. *Coris formosa* is a very similar fish with a black spot on the dorsal fin. The clown labrid *(C. aygula)*, another favorite, also shows color changes as it matures. All *Coris* species are cleaners, picking parasites from other fishes when young, and all mentioned can grow very large, but not too quickly.

Coris gaimard, the clown wrasse, displaying adult coloration while having yet to attain full adult size. A very attractive fish although it can grow quite large.

At the top of this photo is the true cleaner wrasse, *Labroides dimidiatus*, shown here with *Halichoeres chrysus*.

The true cleaner wrasse *(Labroides dimidiatus)* stays quite small and acts as a cleaner all its life. It is important in nature because of this habit and has been shown to keep areas of a reef well populated and healthy. Big fishes like groupers hover in the water to allow the cleaner to do its work. It is a tough fish once acclimated but touchy at first. Naturally, in the aquarium it needs feeding on animal foods.

The rainbow wrasse *(Thalassoma amblycephalus)* and other so-called parrot wrasses are very colorful and variegated in pattern. They feed for preference on small invertebrates and will bite off bits of coral to get at them; but they will adapt to a meaty diet, or even to dried food. The lyretail wrasse *(T. lunare)* is a particular favorite, purple and green in color.

The genus *Halichoeres* has some real beauties, rather rarely seen for sale. They are rather thick-bodied labrids; most grow rather large but are well worth keeping. The saddled rainbow fish *(H. margaritaceous)* and the clouded rainbow fish *(H. nebulosus)* are just as labeled, bearing practically any color you care to mention.

The hogfishes (*Bodianus* species) present a spectrum of colors (reds, yellows, purples, and blues) and undergo the usual color changes. Their one drawback is that most species can grow large and predatory on invertebrates. The Cuban hogfish *(B. pulchellus)* and the Spanish hogfish *(B. rufus)* are cleaners when young but later change to a preferred diet of crustaceans, bivalve mollusks, and echinoderms. In the aquarium they do well on any meaty diet.

The beakfish *(Gomphosus varius)* is a handsome wrasse. Males are bright green and females brown. Unlike most wrasses, it is omnivorous and does well on a mixed diet. It is also a jumper, so beware!

The razorfishes (genus *Hemipteronotus*) are members of the family Labridae, burying themselves in the sand either much of the time or at night. The sargassum razorfish *(H. taeniurus)* looks fragile and can disappear in a clump of weed, but it shoots down into the gravel with alacrity when chased. Other species are blunt-headed, more "normal" looking fishes that offer a variety of colors and color stages during growth.

Pomacanthidae

The angelfishes offer a wonderful selection of quite hardy fishes that come in a wide range of sizes and colors. The smaller ones are well suited to medium-sized aquaria, but the larger species need plenty of room. In nature, they feed on sponges, bryozoa, and other live foods, but fortunately accept most frozen foods and even some dried foods in the aquarium. When juvenile, they are plankton feeders.

Facing Page: The Koran, or semicircle, angelfish (*Pomacanthus semicirculatus*) is a beautifully attractive juvenile, but it grows into a fairly drab adult of around 16 inches.

The genus *Centropyge* contains most of the smaller angels, growing at most to four inches (ten cm). An exception is *C. bicolor*, the blue and gold angelfish, that is at once beautiful, grows quite large, and is difficult to keep. Of the others, and there are many species, the dusky angelfish *(C. bispinosus)*, the lemonpeel angelfish *(C. flavissimus)*, the golden angelfish *(C. heraldi)*, and the flaming angelfish *(C. loriculus)* are particularly recommended. All are colorful and easy to keep. In another genus, Lamarck's angelfish *(Genicanthus lamarck)*, is a nice contrast in black and light gray.

The genus *Pomacanthus* houses many of the larger angels, most of which undergo spectacular color changes as they mature. Some that are quite differently patterned as adults are confusingly similar when young. The semi-circle angelfish *(P. semicirculatus)* when young has white stripes on a blue background, but grows into a rather drab adult up to 16 inches (40 cm) long. The emperor angelfish *(P. imperator)* also has white stripes on a blue background, but these stripes form complete circles centrally, and grows up to be magnificent, with horizontal yellow stripes. The blue ring angelfish *(P. annularis)* has nearly vertical white strips on blue and becomes an adult with blue stripes on a brownish background! These are all Pacific angels.

The Atlantic angels of the same genus *(Pomacanthus)* when young have yellow stripes on a black background and the two common species, the gray angelfish *(P. arcuatus)* and the French angelfish *(P. paru)* are virtually indistinguishable. The adults are quite similar as well and both grow large, with a gray or blackish color and yellow edges on their scales. Other Atlantic angels come from the genus *Holocanthus*. Some are beautiful as adults, particularly the queen angelfish *(H. ciliaris)* and the blue angelfish *(H. isabelita)*. The juveniles are very similar, with blue vertical bars. The rock beauty *(H. tricolor)* is a very popular species, hardy and slow-growing—an advantage since all of these angels get to 12 inches (30 cm) or more eventually! The genus *Euxiphipops* includes two of the most sought-after angelfishes, the blue-girdled angelfish *(E. navarchus)* and the yellow-faced angelfish *(E. xanthometapon)*. Both

Pomacanthus annularis, the blue ring angelfish.

are somewhat less hardy than most angels, but are well worth housing in a reasonably large tank. They can grow to 12 inches (30 cm) or more like the Pomacanthids.

Finally, I must mention another spectacular angel, *Pygoplites diacanthus*, the royal empress angelfish, in order to warn of its difficult nature. Few survive in captivity; they refuse to eat sufficient amounts of anything to keep alive.

Chaetodontidae

The chaetodons, or marine butterflyfishes, are an extensive group. Most are found in the genus *Chaetodon*. Some are quite easy to keep; many need special care; and a few are

Pomacanthus semicirculatus, like many chaetodons, is kept as a juvenile because of its remarkable coloration when young.

nearly impossible. It is important with most of them to select two to four inch (five to ten cm) specimens, for real juveniles need constant live foods and near-adults are specialist feeders. Tank conditions are also important—include a high temperature around 81°F (28°C), a high specific gravity around 1.023 (equals 1.026 at 60°F or 15°C), and well-aerated, pure water. Particularly at first, plenty of live foods are important, but you can expect the majority to become, with time, less fussy concerning both food and water conditions. Mysis shrimps are a favorite with any chaetodon and should always be offered if other foods are refused.

Among the more easily kept species are the sunburst butterflyfish *(C. kleinii)* and the red-striped butterflyfish *(C. lunula).* They rarely refuse to settle in rapidly even in a community tank. Others nearly as obliging are the latticed butterflyfish

(*C. rafflesii*), the threadfin butterflyfish *(C. auriga)*, the four-eyed butterflyfish *(C. capistratus)*, and others. It is a rare chaetodon that is not worth keeping.

Difficult species include the redfin butterflyfish *(C. trifasciatus)*, the Pakistani butterflyfish *(C. collaris)*, and others. Two of the most beautiful chaetodons are the most difficult of all, Meyer's butterflyfish *(C. meyeri)* and the ornate butterflyfish *(C. ornatissimus)*.

The genus *Coradion* closely resembles the *Chaetodons* and is becoming better known as collectors widen their efforts. The coradion butterflyfish *(C. chrysozonus)* is quite attractive, but the best member of the genus, unfortunately rare, is the high-fin *(C. altivelis)*, which looks rather like a cross between a chaetodon and a batfish.

Meyer's butterflyfish, *Chaetodon meyeri*, is a very beautiful but difficult to keep fish, mostly because it is a very selective eater.

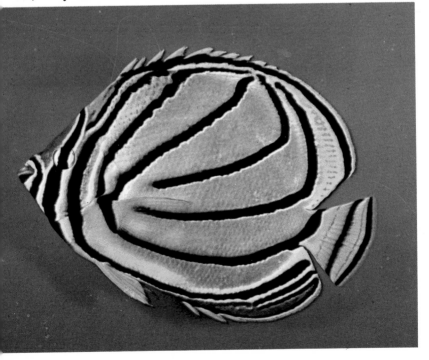

Acanthurus lineatus is usually referred to as the clown surgeonfish; this photo shows a small juvenile. Like all other tangs, it should be fed a good supply of vegetable foods.

The genus *Forcipiger* includes a favorite, *F. longirostris*, the long-nosed butterflyfish. Its long snout is adapted to rummaging out small creatures among the coral, but it is readily acclimatised to the usual aquarium foods. Another fish of similar habits is the copperband butterflyfish *(Chelmon rostratus)*, less ready to accept aquarium foods, but able to do so through a little coaxing with marine live foods or slivers of clam. Both are beautiful fishes. In contrast, the genus *Heniochus* has a number of attractive species that are real gluttons and easy to feed from the beginning. The banner or wimple fish *(H. acuminatus)* has a long, trailing dorsal fin and body pattern rather like a Moorish Idol *(Zanclus canescens)* and is in consequence often called the poor man's Moorish Idol. The Moorish Idol is not a chaetodon, and is one of the hardest fishes to keep, easily infected and hard to feed. This is a great pity, as it is a handsome fish, thus following the usual rule that the nicer they are, the more difficult they are.

Acanthuridae

These are the surgeonfishes or tangs, so-called be-cause they have knife-like protruberances at the base of the tail that can be erected to do severe damage to other fishes or their owner. They are also vegetarians and must be given the right diet to thrive. A good substitute for algae is frozen lettuce or spinach which goes ''gooey'' when thawed and is readily eaten by most surgeons. As they are rather large when fully grown and are very active fishes, the surgeonfishes should be given plenty of room.

There are two outstanding tangs, the powder-blue sur-geon *(Acanthurus leucosternon)* and the blue surgeon *(Para-canthurus hepatus)*. The first is a beautiful pastel blue with a

Tangs, while beautiful fish, will feast on living rock. If you wish to have a living rock structure in your tank, tangs may not be the fish for you. Shown here is *Acanthurus japonicus.*

The sailfin tang, *Zebrasoma veliferum,* has magnificent dorsal and anal fins when young, but tends to lose them as it matures.

yellow dorsal fin and is regrettably rather touchy, although it is alleged that those caught in shallow waters do well, whereas those from deep waters do not. The second is a hardy, deep blue fish with black markings; it will clean up the algae in your aquarium whether you want it to or not. Buy it when it is quite tiny and watch it grow! The clown surgeon *(Acanthurus lineatus)* is another spectacular species, but it shares with the others a capacity to get too large for a medium tank.

   In other genera, the unicorn fish *(Naso lituratus)* with its trailing caudal filaments is quite attractive, but the prize goes to the *Zebrasoma* species. The sailfin tang *(Z. veliferum)* has magnificent dorsal and anal fins when young, and the yellow tang *(Z. flavescens)* is a hardy fish that is bright yellow all over. The young of the brown tang *(Z. scopas)* have large fins and are attractively colored, but the adults are not so nice to look at.

   Some of the surgeonfishes, particularly the blue surgeon, are likely to horrify the aquarist by feigning death when first placed in the aquarium. They lay flat on the bottom and should be left strictly alone; they will soon recover.

Platacidae

The batfishes, so-called because of their long fins, present a problem to the aquarist who has not a large tank in which to house them, preferably by themselves. They are most attractive when young but grow fast. They are nipped by many other fishes and seem to have little defence against it. They range in adaptability from easy to rather difficult.

The orbiculate batfish *(Platax orbicularis)* is the toughest of those commonly available and readily becomes a household pet, although it needs meaty foods and often refuses dried foods. It gets to know its owner and will take food from the

Platax pinnatus is a very attractive but less than hardy fish. You need a deep tank and a lot of experience to expect success with this batfish.

hand. Its one drawback is its growth rate!

The long-finned batfish *(P. pinnatus)* is not as hardy as *P. orbicularis* but is a real beauty when young. Unfortunately the bright red edges running around the fish fade off with growth, which can be to 18 inches (45 cm) in length and even more in depth. This is not a fish for the beginner or for anyone without a large, deep tank.

Also called the long-finned batfish, *P. teira* really deserves the name. Although it has not the spectacular colors of *P. pinnatus*, its depth, particularly when young, is astonishing. Like its namesake, it is a somewhat touchy fish and must be given live or frozen meaty foods such as fish, clam, or earthworms. It can grow to 24 inches (60 cm) in favorable circumstances! If you decide to keep batfishes, keep them hungry and remember that a fish on a restricted diet, as long as it is nutritious, can be kept down in size without suffering in any way.

Balistidae

The triggerfishes get their name from an erectile spike, part of the anterior dorsal fin, that can be locked into place at will. Sometimes there is a similar ventral spike. If the fish dives into a coral head and erects the spike or spikes, it can be impossible to dislodge it uninjured. The group as a whole is distinguished by toughness and aggression, but there are some exceptions. In nature, they are predatory fishes, eating crustaceans, echinoderms and even mollusks. They can turn a spiny sea urchin over and attack its underside or crunch through a mussel shell. In the aquarium, they readily accept any meaty food.

The clown triggerfish *(Balistoides conspicillum* or *B. niger)* is world famous as a spectacular exhibit in public aquaria. Until recently only large specimens were available, but quite small juveniles are for sale today—at a price, because they can more readily be kept in home aquaria, but they do grow. Although I have known large specimens to be kept in community tanks, it is a rare happening, as *B. conspicillum* is a nasty-tempered rogue and quite untrustworthy. It will attack at random, bite through airlines and heater cables and even rearrange the seascape to its own liking. It can grow to 20 inches (50 cm).

An adult clown triggerfish, *Balistoides conspicillum*, is an imposing fish that can grow to 20 inches.

The pink-tailed triggerfish *(Melichthys vidua)* is another beauty that you can actually hope to keep with other fishes, although it can grow as large as *B. conspicillum*. It is not too aggressive and becomes very tame, taking food from the hand—but be careful, it can mistake your fingers for a delicious morsel. Its close relative, the black-finned triggerfish *(M. indicus)*, is a less peaceful but handsome fish of quite variable body coloration from orange to off-white with, of course, black fins.

The black triggerfish *(Odonus niger)* is a much better bet. Growing only to about eight inches (20 cm), it is safe with all but really shy tank-mates and is a striking, all-black or all-

blue fish—there seem to be two strains, and both have red teeth! Another fish of similar temperament and size is the blue-lined trigger *(Pseudobalistes fuscus)*. It is very beautiful, but unfortunately rare and expensive.

A favorite fish from Hawaii, when small, is the Picasso fish *(Rhineacanthus aculeatus)*, who rejoices in the native name of humu-humu-nuku-nuku-a-puaa. A two inch (five cm) specimen is pretty and quite peaceful, but it is a fast grower and becomes increasingly nasty. Choose a tiny one and you can enjoy it for a year or so.

Two striking triggerfishes, both aggressive but worth keeping in a tank of their own, are the undulate trigger *(Balistapus undulatus)* and the queen trigger *(Balistes vetula)*. They are

The triggerfishes get their name from an erectile spike that is a part of their anterior dorsal fin, clearly displayed here on *Balistes vetula*.

From the family Monacanthidae come the filefishes. They are attractive but can prove overly selective feeders. Shown here is *Pervagor spilosoma*.

great furniture removalists and so should be given an aquarium with heavy rocks or corals and well-hidden airlines or heater cords, or better still, one with a divided arrangement so that the exhibition area has no equipment in it.

Lutjanidae

The sea perches or snappers of the genus *Lutjanus* are kept as juveniles only, since many reach up to 36 inches (90 cm) or so as adults. Those from inshore are mostly green and spotted or banded, whereas those from deeper waters are red. They are carnivores and tend to be voracious feeders in the aquarium, preferring live foods but eating anything suitable.

The blood-red snapper *(L. sanguineus)* is a bright rose-pink with stripes when young and less attractive later, when it is too big for a home aquarium anyway. The blue-striped snapper *(L. kasmira)* is bright yellow with blue bands and has the advantage of growing only to 12 inches (30 cm). The well-known red emperor *(L. sebae)* is unfortunately only red as a near-adult of two or three feet (60-90 cm), and is brownish and white when young.

In other genera, the red-bellied fusilier *(Caesio erythro-gaster)* is a remarkable fish with a blue back, red belly and yel-

The harlequin sweetlips, *Plectorhynchus chaetodonoides*, is also known as the polkadot grunt. It is a popular and well colored fish.

low forked tail, growing to about 12 inches (30 cm), while the blue-banded whiptail *(Pentapodus setosus)* is another beauty attaining about the same size. In the genus *Plectorhynchus* or sweetlips is a variety of species of striking colors that often change considerably in pattern as they mature to a length of around 24 inches (60 cm). Those most familiar are the polka-dot grunt *(P. chaetodonoides)* and the striped sweetlips *(Gaterin lineatus)*. The polka-dot is a difficult feeder, whereas the striped sweetlips is not. The related emperorfishes (genus *Lethrinus*) offer a range of rarely imported but colorful species closely resembling the snapper in habits, size and appearance.

Holocentridae

The squirrelfishes and soldierfishes are on the whole smaller than the snappers; they are mostly reddish in color, and are often quite attractive. Their large eyes give a clue to their nocturnal habits. They are also fierce predators and not safe with fishes they can eat. All of which indicates that they are

hardly suitable to a small community tank! Nevertheless, they are kept by aquarists having a tank with suitable inmates. They learn to eat meaty foods, but most will rarely take them unless they can see them falling through the water.

The genus *Adioryx* contains a number of species that are kept, of which the reef squirrelfish *(A. coruscus)* is perhaps the best, not growing large and looking attractive. The dusky squirrelfish *(A. vexillarius)* is another one of the smaller species often kept in the home aquarium. The genus *Flammeo* is duller in color, but its members are easier to feed, some even accepting dried foods. The blood-spot squirrelfish *(F. sammara)* is attractive and easy to keep. The genus *Myripristis*, often referred to as soldierfishes, is more choosy, but the red soldierfish *(M. pralinius)* is so showy that it is a popular fish. Like all squirrelfishes, it should be given plenty of hiding places and preferably subdued lighting.

Apogonidae

The cardinalfishes are a large family of rather perchlike fishes and are found in many parts of the tropics. Some have oral gestation, with the male usually carrying the eggs.

Seale's cardinalfish, *Apogon sealei*, remains quite small and has a delicate and attractive color.

Some penetrate brackish or even fresh water, and many are brilliantly colored, with red predominating. They are quite hardy and can be recommended to the beginner, even though they are reluctant to accept other than live food at first and rarely graduate to dried foods.

Kuhliidae

The flag-tails, or reef trout, are strongly laterally compressed fishes within a single genus, *Kuhlia*. Some are found in fresh water as well as in the sea. The reef trout *(K. taeniura)* is said to be about the toughest fish available, known to survive in a gallon jar for several months and in the Steinhard Aquarium for ten years. Young specimens have a plain silvery body and a decorated tail. The very similar Aholehole *(K. sandvicensis)* of Hawaii is equally worth keeping, while the Queensland rock flag-tail *(K. rupestris)* is equally at home in fresh water.

The tiny Catalina goby, *Lythrypnus dalli*, is a hardy, brightly marked, temperate water marine fish that will also do well in the heated aquarium.

Fishes

Gobiidae

The gobies and gudgeons are a mixed bag of mostly small fishes that may inhabit fresh or salt water, and sometimes both. They are common in rock pools and shallow estuaries (muddy or sandy), where they feed on animal matter of one kind or another. Most are not especially colorful, but they are mostly peaceful, hardy and suitable for mixed communities. The well-known mudskippers (*Periophthalmus* and other genera) make interesting pets, but they need a vivarium rather than an aquarium so that they may leave the water when they feel like it.

The neon goby *(Gobiosoma oceanops)* is perhaps the best-known of the family. It comes from the tropical Atlantic, where it acts as a cleaner very much like the Pacific cleaner wrasse *(Labroides dimidiatus)*, which it somewhat resembles. It and other members of the genus *Gobiosoma* are very interesting little fishes, often associated with the red corals or with sponges. In the aquarium, it will feed on live foods, frozen brine shrimp, or mysis shrimps.

The lemon goby *(Gobiodon citrinus)* is an attractive, laterally compressed fish that may be green or brown rather than lemon-yellow. It lives in the branches of corals and adapts well to aquarium life.

The tiny Catalina goby *(Lythrypnus dalli)*, from the island of that name off the California coast, is a gem, and although really a temperate water fish, it survives surprisingly well in the tropical aquarium.

Various *Ptereleotris* species are becoming available in quantity and are now classed with the gobies. Having lost the typical sucking disc of the family, they were at first separated from it. The fire fish (originally *P. splendidum*, now *Nemateleotris magnificus*) is indeed both splendid and magnificent! The scissortail *(P. tricolor)* is another fine member of the genus. The gudgeons, similarly, have separate ventral fins but are placed in the subfamily Eleotrinae. Many live in fresh water, and the ocean-dwelling species are rarely kept. However, the lined gudgeon *(Calleleotris muralis)* is a very pretty little fish that stays small and attractive.

Ecsenius fourmanoiri is another member of the blenny family. It is small and attractive, having the unusual body structure typical of the blennies.

Blenniidae

The blennies are mostly small carnivorous fishes distributed from the Arctic to the tropics and of very many genera. They have no scales and usually have slender bodies, inhabiting tide-pools and shallow coastal waters. Some species bear living young. The oyster blenny *(Petroscirtes anolius)* is a pretty little fish not seen in aquaria very often. It mates when small, and the pair then enter the shell of a dead oyster from which they cannot later escape, feeding on whatever chance brings them.

The genus *Ecsenius* has some colorful members, of which the bicolor blenny *(E. bicolor)* is a good example, purple in front and orange behind. It will eat vegetable or meaty food and makes a good aquarium fish. The rock blenny *(E. pulcher)* is another common species, also bicolored, slate-blue in front and yellow at the rear. The genus *Meiacanthus* rivals the fore-

going, with a number of attractive species such as the forktail blenny *(M. atrodorsalis)* and the brilliant canary blenny *(M. atrodorsalis oualanensis)*, also a forktailed fish, but just bright yellow all over.

The genus *Blennius* is well known for the molly miller *(B. cristatus)* with its crested head. It is a pity that the large variety of Mediterranean blennies in this genus are not more easily captured and made available, as there are some spectacular species. If ever you see specimens of the horned blenny *(B. tentacularis)*, the carmine blenny *(B. nigriceps)* or the peacock blenny *(B. pavo)* for sale, grab them! On the other hand, attractive as they are, avoid purchasing any of the saber-toothed blennies (*Plagiotremus* species), as they are scale and fin nippers, subsisting in nature on chunks bitten from other fishes.

Callionymidae

The dragonets are small and colorful fishes from both temperate and tropical seas, usually with spectacular males and

Small in size yet rich in color, *Synchiropus splendidus* is a gem to behold in the marine aquarium.

A partner in beauty to *S. splendidus* is *S. picturatus*, also known as the psychedelic fish.

somewhat less impressive females. The males typically have larger fins and are bigger and more colorful than their mates, which they court in an elaborate fashion, rather rarely seen in the marine fishes, finishing with a scattering of eggs and sperm into the upper layers of the water.

The genus *Synchiropus* supplies two of the best-known dragonets, the mandarinfish *(S. splendidus)* and the psychedelic fish *(S. picturatus)*. The mandarinfish, with its tapestry-like markings, is hard to beat for unique appearance and beauty. Unfortunately it is also hard to keep unless in the company of other slow and deliberate feeders like seahorses or pipefishes. In a community it is liable to starve, as it slowly searches around the tank for choice morsels, inspecting each carefully before eating it. Meanwhile, the other fishes gobble it all down! The psychedelic fish, on the contrary, is a less choosy

Fishes

feeder and can usually hold its own against other fishes, but really fares best if kept with slow feeders. Both will exhibit their mating behavior in the aquarium.

Other species less often seen are the fingered dragonet *(Dactylopus dactylopus)*, with a gloriously high-finned and colorful male and an attractive female, and the ornate dragonet from Japan, *(Callionymus calliste)*, another beauty, also found in Australia.

Tetraodontidae

Together with the following two families, the Tetraodontidae make up a sub-order of very similar fishes, the Tetraodontoidei. They all have more or less inflatable bellies and are more or less poisonous, being responsible for many deaths each year in the Orient. The pufferfishes, or toados, have scaleless, often prickly skins and can blow themselves up with air or water when attacked. The poison they carry is a tasteless and odorless alkaloid.

Pufferfishes are odd-looking, generally attractive fishes that are commonly kept in the hobby. Shown here is *Canthigaster callisterna*.

The genus *Sphoeroides* has a number of colorful members, among which the banded toado *(S. pleurostictus)*, with its bright orange-red fins, is perhaps the most spectacular small fish. Some others of the genus grow to two or three feet (60-90 cm). The genus *Tetraodon* has some very colorful species, but they also grow too large.

Canthigasteridae

This is a family of small pufferfishes with long snouts and a single genus, *Canthigaster*. Most are colorful and make good aquarium fishes, *except* for the capacity of many species to poison the whole tank, including themselves, if unduly disturbed. Many an aquarist has collected a bucket full of fishes from the ocean and found all dead on getting them home because of a single pufferfish. They are ready feeders on almost any of the usual aquarium foods.

Practically all of the commonly available sharp-nosed puffers are called just that, being distinguished most often by

The four-barred toby, *Canthigaster coronata*. Puffers are capable of releasing a poison that can kill not only other fishes but also themselves. Discretion must be exercised with these unusual animals.

Diodon hystrix, the porcupinefish, is common in the aquarium trade and accessible to the hobbyist.

their places of origin. The "common" sharp-nosed puffer is *C. valentini*, widespread in the Indo-Pacific and an attractive fish. The Red Sea sharp-nosed puffer *(C. margaritatus)* and the Hawaiian sharp-nosed puffer *(C. jactator)* are both white-spotted on a dark background, both small, up to three or four inches (7½-10 cm) and both regularly sold. The Israeli puffer *(C. coronata)* is another small and odd-looking fish that carries its body at an angle with a squinched-up tail, looking sick even when it is not.

Diodontidae

In addition to inflatability, the porcupinefishes have spines covering the body that stick out when the fish blows itself up, rendering it even less edible than the puffers. Most of them grow large, but small specimens are often kept as a curiosity, although it is not a kindness to demonstrate their ability to puff up too frequently. Those full of air sometimes seem unable to deflate and float helplessly in the water.

The common porcupinefish *(Diodon hystrix)* is found all over the tropical seas and is the one usually available. A similar but smaller and rather less spiny fish is *Tragulichthys jaculiferus*, common around Australia.

Ostraciontidae

The boxfishes, or trunkfishes, and cowfishes have the body enclosed in six-sided bony plates that are fused together and quite rigid. There are some attractive species, many with poisonous flesh and some capable of producing toxins that will kill off other fishes including themselves, as with some of the pufferfishes.

One of the most popular boxfishes, the spotted boxfish *(Ostracion meleagris)* has this ability and should be treated with

Like some of the pufferfishes, many boxfishes can release toxins capable of killing themselves and others. Shown is *Ostracion meleagris*, the spotted boxfish.

Lionfishes present a dual threat to other fishes in your aquarium: they will eat any other fish that they are capable of swallowing, and they have poisonous dorsal spines. Pictured here is *Pterois antennata* (the spotfin lionfish).

caution; in fact, it is best avoided. The male has orange spots and the female has white ones. The spotted cube *(Ostracion cubicus)* is also popular and has not been accused of poisoning the water. Boxfishes are carnivorous and readily accept a meaty diet.

The cowfishes, so-called because of their spines above the eyes, make nice pets when young, but can grow quite large. The scrawled cowfish *(Lactophrys quadricornis)* and the long-horned cowfish *(Lactoria cornuta)* are good aquarium fishes and make interesting pets, becoming quite tame.

Scorpaenidae

The lionfishes, turkeyfishes or butterfly cod, are magnificent creatures with two drawbacks. They will eat anything they can swallow in the way of other fishes or crustaceans and they have poisonous dorsal spines. Otherwise, they are easy to keep and do not molest other large fishes. When first acquired, a lionfish will eat only live prey, but particularly if kept hungry

it soon learns to eat dead fishes or chunks of meat, prawn, or fish. It is best taught to do this by impaling the food on a needle-tipped stick and waving it in front of the fish. Later, it will feed from the hand—but be careful of the poisonous spines! Small specimens deliver painful but relatively harmless wounds, but larger ones can debilitate or even kill. The venom is a neurotoxin. The much-feared stonefish *(Synanceja horrida)* is a member of this family and lies concealed among coral or in mudflats to be trodden upon by the unwary, and it often kills its victim.

The genus *Pterois* gives us a group of popular lion fishes, the best-known being the common lionfish *(P. volitans)*. It has large, feathery pectoral fins, a striped, ferocious-looking body and head, and long dorsal spines. In the wild, it herds its prey by spreading the pectorals and trapping it in a convenient spot among the coral. Very young specimens are almost colorless and may grow up into the common red-brown variety or into a darker type, sometimes almost black. If fed liberally they grow rapidly. It is best to keep them a little short of food, as they can attain a length of 15 inches (37 cm).

Dendrochirus zebra, the zebra lionfish, closely resembles some *Pterois* sp.

This photo clearly shows the shorter fins of *Dendrochirus zebra* as compared to those of many *Pterois sp.*.

My own favorite among the *Pterois* species is the whitefin lionfish *(P. radiata)* with its white-striped body and pectorals. It is nocturnal and shy at first, and harder to feed than *P. volitans,* but soon becomes good and gets to know its owner. The somewhat similar spotfin lionfish *(P. antennata)* has double white bars on the body and more feathery pectorals. The *P. sphex* comes from Hawaii and looks somewhat like *P. antennata.*

The genus *Dendrochirus* contains shorter-finned but still very attractive fishes. Their habits are much the same as *Pterois* and they are also poisonous. The zebra lionfish *(D. zebra)* is like a dwarf *P. antennata,* with the pectoral rays connected like a fan. Another species, *D. brachypterus,* is more common to pet shops and is very attractive. There are 20 or 30 other genera, many with attractive and usually poisonous members.

Serranidae

The genus *Serranus* contains some small, even tiny members, such as the lantern bass *(S. baldwini)* that grows only to about two and a half inches (six cm) and is a common aquarium fish from the tropical Atlantic. Other *Serranus* species grow to enormous sizes. The tobacco fish *(S. tabacarius)* is also quite small for a serranid, but is not very colorful or popular. The harlequin bass *(S. tigrinus)* on the other hand is equally small, yet a pretty, desirable fish.

Perhaps the most popular when small is the golden striped grouper *(Grammistes sexlineatus)*. It makes a good aquarium fish if with sizeable companions, but has rivals in the genus *Cephalopholis*. The black grouper *(C. argus)* is a variably colored species, choice specimens having blue spots on a very dark body. The red grouper *(C. miniatus)* is similarly spotted on a red body. Both grow to about 16 inches (40 cm). The Boenacki grouper *(C. boenack)* has blue stripes and is a favorite. It and the golden striped grouper produce a toxic slime that discourages other fishes from eating them.

The genus *Epinephelus* provides some further beauties, of which the most outstanding is the blue and yellow grouper *(E. flavocaeruleus)*, whose pastel-blue body rivals the powder-blue surgeon *(Acanthurus leucosternon)*. Other desirable juveniles are the red hind *(E. guttatus)* and the rock cods *E. hexagonatus* and *E. merra*, the white speckled rock cod and the honeybomb grouper.

Of the remaining groupers that are kept when small, mention must be made of the polka-dot grouper *(Chromileptes altivelis)*. When young, it has large black spots on a silvery-grey body and a tiny head; it is amazingly self-possessed and tame. It grows to 26 inches (65 cm) and loses its attractiveness to become a top-line food fish, as are many groupers.

In another subfamily lie the hamlets *(Hypoplectrus* species), chunky fishes from the west Atlantic, of which the most attractive is the golden hamlet *(H. gummigutta)*, unfortunately a rare species. The most common is the barred hamlet *(H. puella)*, less beautiful but still worth having. The shy hamlet *(H. guttavarius)* is also rare and like a clouded golden hamlet in appearance, while the butter hamlet *(H. unicolor)* is fairly unin-

The family Serranidae contains many small species; the coral rockcod, *Cephalophis miniatus*, however, is not one of them. Although a very attractive fish, it can grow to about 16 inches.

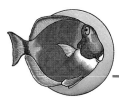

viting. All appear to be carnivorous and very similar except for color; all reach about five inches (12½ cm) in length.

Grammidae

The basslets live in caves and under ledges in shallow or deep water and thus are not easy to collect. Once available, they become good aquarium fishes but do tend to hide away. They are carnivorous fishes.

The fairy basslet *(Gramma loreto)* is a great favorite, growing only to three inches (7½ cm), and is frequently sold as the royal gramma. It has a more uniformly colored cousin, the blackcap basslet *(G. melacara)*. The candy basslet *(Liopropoma carmabi)* is an even smaller fish than the fairy basslet, while its

Gramma loreto, the royal gramma, is an ideal fish for the hobbyist. It grows to only about three inches and has a purple and yellow coloration.

The most commonly kept genus of sea horse is *Hippocampus*. Sea horses like *H. kuda* (shown here) are commonly caught off Hawaii.

close relative, the Swissguard basslet *(L. rubre)* is a bit larger. As with the other basslets, they hide their beauty rather too effectively.

Syngnathidae

The pipefishes and seahorses are fascinating creatures, especially the latter, but should only be kept if a supply of suitable live food can be maintained or, in some cases, a supply of frozen mysis shrimps, a food they have been found to accept. They are armoured fishes in which the male has a brood-pouch

formed of folds of skin that meet on the underside of the tail or abdomen. After mating rituals that some will perform in the aquarium, the female inserts the eggs into the pouch where they are kept until the young are released and free-swimming. The young of at least some of the smaller seahorses can be raised on newly-hatched brine shrimp and will accept them for life, whereas their parents would not necessarily do so.

There are many genera of pipefishes, some even found in fresh water, but most are strictly marine. The genus *Doryramphus* has the most colorful species, including the zebra pipefish *(D. dactyliophorus)*, with a black-striped body and a red tail. The banded pipefish *(Yozia tigris)* has reddish dark bands on the body but no red tail.

There are many genera of seahorses, some highly colored and many less remarkable, but none measure up to the oceanic genera *Phycodurus* and *Phyllopteryx*, the sea dragons. Some are brilliantly colored, some having a leafy appearance due to numerous appendages. With their upright stance and curious swimming motion, even the ordinary seahorses are unique, live well if properly cared for and can quite easily be bred.

A commonly kept genus is *Hippocampus*, having a world-wide distribution. Most species are black, brown, or yellor in color, with a degree of adaptability to match their surroundings. The oceanic seahorse *(H. kuda)* is an attractive yellow and is caught off Hawaii. The Northern seahorse *(H. erectus)* is dark brown and comes from the western Atlantic; its eastern Atlantic counterparts are *H. hippocampus* and *H. brevirostris* (the short-snouted sea horses). For more color, we must go to the Japanese crowned sea horse *(H. coronatus)*, with red patches on head and body, or to *H. mohnikei*, also from Japan, that is red all over. Another beauty, *H. bargibanti*, is blue and red when it is on a suitable background, but is capable of remarkable color changes.

Antennariidae

Anglerfishes are found in practically all seas and vary in size from a few inches to several feet; but, only the tropical species provide colorful and suitably sized aquarium fishes.

Hippocampus angustatus, the tigersnout seahorse.

Suitable, that is, to a tank with larger fishes than the anglers, for those smaller will disappear with alacrity. Large anglers will even eat small anglers, and not much smaller than themselves at that. The characteristic feature of an angler is the bait—a modified dorsal spine looking like a tasty morsel and in some species waved about in wriggling activity. Deep-sea anglers have them illuminated.

World-wide in warm seas is the sargassum fish *(Histrio histrio)* that floats beautifully camouflaged in the weed of that name. Like most anglers, it can be trained to take dead food by dangling it in front of the fish, but one then misses the fascinating baiting and capture. Most aquarium species belong to the genus *Antennarius*, found in shallow water and easily captured. They come in a great range of colors and patterns. The striped angler *(A. striatus)* may drift in weeds like the sargassum fish, but is also found stalking along the bottom of harbours and inlets. There are several red species: the longlure angler *(A. multiocellatus)* from the Atlantic, the red anglers *(A. sanguineus,*

The sargassum fish *(Histrio histrio)* is an exotic looking fish that can be a joy to your hobby. Care must be taken, for they will eat almost anything that they can swallow—including other sargassum fish.

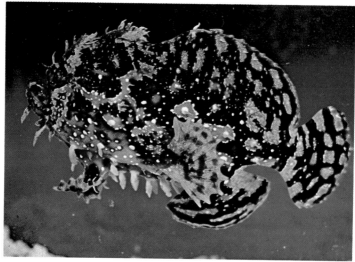

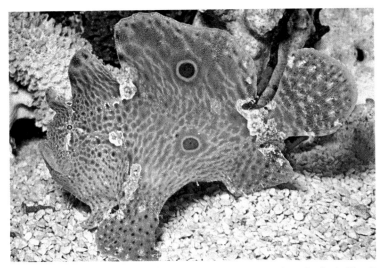

Antennarius ocellatus, the ocellated frogfish, is commonly kept in the hobby. It is interesting to watch it lure its prey by waving the appendage above its eyes.

A. nummifer, and *A. pictus)* from the Pacific, and others. The black angler *(A. moluccensis)* and a black variety of the striped angler which may change color to yellow when placed in the aquarium, are other Pacific varieties.

Many of the above-mentioned anglers are easy to spawn in captivity, when the female after a chase by the male lays vast numbers of eggs in a long, coiled mass of jelly. Although these will hatch in a few days, I have not succeeded in or seen a report of the raising of the fry. It would be fascinating to obtain a female of one of the smaller deep-sea anglers to see how reproduction occurs, since the tiny male latches onto the female when he comes across her and acts as a parasite from then on, sharing her circulation and nourishment.

Sciaenidae

The genera *Equetus* and *Eques* are both called high hats because of the long dorsal fin and offer various attractive striped fishes. The cubbyu *(Eques acuminatus)* is the most usual high-hat, while the jackknife fish *(Equetus lanceolatus)* comes from deeper water and is not so often available.

Monocentridae

The pineconefishes are oddities, with the body covered by bony scales that are bright yellow with black edges. One species *(Monocentrus japonicus)* has been a rare treasure at a few public aquaria, but the Australian species *(Monocentrus gloria-maris)* is sometimes on sale and is said to be unique in having bright scarlet patches on the lower lip, one each side, that are luminous and can be left covered or exposed. This fish comes from deep waters and presumably hunts with their aid. It is caught in fair numbers by prawn trawlers and grows to nine inches (22 cm).

Monodactylidae

Fishes with a plethora of names (Malayan angel, diamondfish, moonfish, silver batfish, butterfish, etc.), the monodactylids are usually called brackish water fishes but in fact can stand anything from the ocean to hard fresh water. The presence of calcium is critical, and they die off in soft water. They are prettiest when small but can grow to nine inches (32 cm).

The Malayan angel *(Monodactylus argenteus)* from the Pacific is a tough but rather shy fish best kept in small groups. It eats practically anything. Its West African relative *(M. sebae)* is a little more tender, but still a hardy and perhaps more attractive fish.

Theraponidae

The grunters, tigerfishes or perches, are also tolerant of salt or fresh waters (euryhaline fishes, as opposed to stenohaline fishes—fishes that cannot stand much of a salinity change). They come in several genera, are generally school fishes, and look best in groups.

The crescent perch *(Therapon jarbua)* is a very active and attractive fish when small, eats anything and is very hardy. Its only disadvantage is that it grows too quickly if well fed and can get to about twelve inches (30 cm). It has some equally attractive relatives that never seem to be kept in aquaria although they are quite common in the wild. The bar-tailed grunter *(T. caudovittatus)* is a handsome fish that does not grow so large as *T. jarbua*, and the trumpeter perch *(Pelates*

quadriliniatus) is similarly worth keeping. I had one by accident in with some *T. jarbua*, which it quite resembles, and it lived on quite happily until it got too large for my tanks.

Scatophagidae

The "scats" or butterfishes are chaetodon-like fishes that also live in salt or fresh water, a most unchaetodon-like capacity. They are believed to breed in estuaries, since the young stages are regularly found there and make good freshwater aquarium pets, staying quite small for a long period. If they are transferred to salt water, their growth is very much accelerated and they lose their attractiveness.

The spotted scat *(Scatophagus argus)* is a muck-eater but is used as a food fish when adult in many communities. The common variety is quite attractive when young, but *S. argus* var. *rubifrons* is bright red dorsally when young and very handsome. This feature disappears with growth. Scats have many spines that can inflict painful wounds and should be handled with care. Juveniles are algae eaters but will take all normal

Scatophagus argus, a scavenger in the wild, is an attractive fish when young.

foods as well.

The other genus in the family, *Selenotoca*, offers a rather similar but less attractive fish, *Selenotoca multifasciata*, found in tropical waters, and *S. multifasciata* var. *aetativarians*, from more temperate waters.

Plesiopidae

Closely related to the pseudochromids are the longfins, small or fairly small carnivores with longish fins, of which the most commonly available to the trade seems to be the comet (*Calloplesiops altivelis*). It is an impressive fish with the appearance of a continuous fin from back to belly when all fins are erect. It is quite at home and no trouble as long as it is with fishes it cannot swallow and not with another comet, as they fight and spoil their beauty. Its cousin, *C. argus*, is sometimes seen and is distinguishable from the comet in having even bigger fins and tail and smaller spots.

Calloplesiops altivelis, the comet, is one of the more spectacularly patterned groupers.

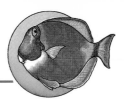

A cousin to *C. altivelis* is *C. argus*, the, argus comet. It has larger fins and smaller spots. It is also very attractive, although less frequently seen than its popular cousin.

Scaridae

Most of the parrotfishes are unfortunately too large for the home aquarium, but as with the groupers, juveniles may prove too attractive to resist and be kept for a period. They are related to the wrasses, but have their teeth fused into a parrot-like beak to a greater or lesser extent. They feed on vegetation, coral, mussels and anything their powerful jaws can crush, and so are not for the minireef type of tank. Their numbers include some of the brightest and most colorful fishes on offer.

The genus *Scarus* offers the princess parrotfish (*S. taeniopterus*), with colorful males and drab females, and *S. sexvittatus* (called simply "parrotfish"), with reddish juveniles and females and blue-and-green males. As with many of the genus, full color in the males is only seen when they are getting too

large—a great pity. Another peculiarity is the common habit of spinning a mucus cocoon in which to spend the night.

The genus *Sparisoma* rivals the above. The red-tail parrotfish *(S. chrysopterum)* is again unfortunate for us in developing good color in the males only in adulthood, but the stoplight parrotfish *(S. viride)* has brightly colored males and females— the former green in the main and the latter with a bright red belly and fins. The most commonly kept parrotfish is the two-colored one *(Bolbometopon bicolor)* because the juveniles are fully colored and change pattern as they grow—to 24 inches (60 cm).

The rusty parrotfish, *Scarus ferrugineus*, like most of the other parrotfishes, is a beautiful fish that will quickly grow too large for the home aquarium.

The following books by T.F.H. Publications are available at pet shops everywhere.

MARINE FISHES AND INVERTEBRATES IN YOUR HOME
By Dr. Cliff W. Emmens
ISBN 0-86622-790-3
TFH H-1103

SUGGESTED READING

Contents: Marine Environment. Some Measurements. Controlling Aquarium Conditions. Biological Filtration. Setting Up Your Marine Aquarium. Buying and Handling Fishes. Feeding Marine Fishes. Diseases and Parasites. The Natural System. Reproduction in Marine Fishes.

Audience: Dr. Cliff W. Emmens is the ultimate authority on marine aquarium keeping, and his unique background as a scientist, university professor and writer proclaim his distinction in this field.

Hard cover, 8½" × 11", 192 pages 315 full-color photos and drawings

Index

Index